White Heat

SARA TROPPER

White Heat

Red Moon Press
PO Box 2461
Winchester VA
22604-1661 USA
www.redmoonpress.com

Cover design David Berger: *Red Haiku* (detail).
Ink and watercolor on paper, 2025.

Second Printing

Dedicated to the victims of October 7

White Heat

6:29
paragliders
in the bright blue

scrambling eggs
for the soldier's children
morning thunder

We open at the close

It was evening, it was morning: the Sabbath day. Everyone wanted to dance. Some had taken Torah scrolls from the Ark, for reading and rotation. Entering the Land and beginning again. Others had encamped in the desert, Nova Festival of Booths.

> late new year
> the ram's horn
> entangled

bomb shelter palms on a pregnant belly

abducted
the pacifier
dangling

sons at war
the new year's
brightest blue

after the storm
the new mathematics . . .
matching body parts

strafed
and still
the light

hitting the high notes
children ape
an air raid siren

piebald sky . . .
the ponies
between bombs

What we have

I am holding his boots, high-topped and heavy. Each eyelet an accusation. The baby kicks.

    war widow
    the light
    of the letter

first day of shiva—
the wail of the baby
without her breast

unmindful
of the border breach
almonds are ripening

adding to my tab
ice cream
for the unknown soldier

blinking in the still dark the bomber the blackbird

hard rain shrapnel on the roof

shaking skies—
the children hopscotch
between broadcasts

afterwards . . .
close enough to kiss
warplanes

shavasana
in a shelter letting go
of the bomb

touchdown already on the tarmac thunder

low-flying fighters
he helps modulate
a haiku

Historical note

In seventeenth-century Amsterdam, a misfit by the name of Spinoza ran afoul of the Jewish authorities for advocating a waiting period before burial.

> midnight spading
> every grave
> more shadow

discussing morality
with the soldier's child
rays of the moon

Har Herzl—
a shortage
of small stones

handcuffed
my bracelet at birth
had another name

absorbing my sorrow your skin

act of God
a mockingbird
outsings the missile

too many tomatoes
on the sideboard
empty nest

godless month praying among the pieces

from afar
lightly
God

Sabbath tea
a small bow
to the stained hands

fractal
the eucalyptus
endlessly rooting

Where we are right

It's new year's so no cell phones as we crisscross Jerusalem, looking for the place. Down this street, up this alley, no one knows and everyone wants to help, absorbing shock waves from the south—in the north, a shofar blast in a bunker. We pause at the bus stop and select a dress, pretty and free-for-the-taking.

    ruined house
    where we were wronged
    dancing

Called on account of war

Three hyrax, butterballed and staring.
The babies behind. They retreat to their rocks as we
move along.

    if the guns are real infiltration

first light
the weight of it . . .
my son's rifle

artillery to the East a starling's circuit

so much and still the sparrow

existential war again the mourning dove

if not one way then another morning river

Ring trilogy

It all started on a black sabbath in October. When the father found out, he wept diamonds. Later, he saw wedding pictures and vowed to set the stones. Now, his son is present at each and every chuppah in the field.

She lost her love and then her ring. The first defending the country, the second at the sea. Facebook blew up looking for his name on a golden band. And then, in Russian, they were inscribed.

Anan is the cloud in which God placed the rainbow of promise: no more destruction, not the whole shebang. He is also the father of Jamal, who rings from Gaza one last time before taking the hit for his platoon. Fourth-generation Druze hero.

    triple yahrzeit
    one year's growth
    of amaryllis

among mourners the soldier's child strolling

rockets to roses
around my neck
shrapnel blooms

קיבוץ מושחר—
חמסה כחולה
תלויה

kibbutz ruins—
blue hamsa eye
hanging

أطلال الكيبوتس –
الخرزة الزرقاء
معلّقة

dayenu under fire the calculus of enough

asleep in the safe room her scarf askew

wartime glads
smiling
at the sword lily

one sister atop another
fledglings
grave to grave

shared syntax
in the bunker
hijab and headscarf

one book
for the bunker
jisei

still trembling after the aftershock wild wheat

rock hyrax
the war wadi
thrumming

suddenly winter
my child
chanting kaddish

checking for life
    the child's doll . . .
cricket moon

still no news
the time it takes . . .
half-life

straddling a hairsbreadth of light

moonlit scat
hugging myself
a little harder

half-light
giving a pep talk
the upper part of a soldier

keeping watch on the wadi thistledown

short drive
racing thunderclouds
to the war

لا شيء سوى الدعاء
في ذكرى المائة يوم
من الشرائط

nothing but a prayer
on this hundredth
day of ribbons

רק תפילה
מאה ימים
של סרטים

work standstill
all the employees
in warrior 1

pointing at parchment
the Jewish soldier
and his hook

Night moves

Hakol b'seder. Everything's okay, I told a passerby
at midnight. He was taking his constitutional,
and I remembered that he'd been knifed once
right around here. So I mouthed the magic
words, the ones everyone in Israel wants to hear
at times like this. At times like this. The police
were packing up; the sidewalk was clean. No
blood where I sat, patting a dog. With a friend
whose child had bolted. Whose child would
awaken, remembering only the urge to run.

    border breach
    the sunrise
    relentless

wildwheat morning
the newscaster confirms
a second front

scattering toward the wind my final face

empty turtle shell
starting to discuss
burial arrangements

deep cicada
the jisei
I don't write

art exhibition
hanging by a thread
the children's faces

lost online the moon rising without me

5 red, 5 round
noticing what's here
and who isn't

recoil forcing myself to face the gun

דממה עד דמעות הפיקוס

quiet until the ficus weeps

صمت لغاية بكاء الفيكس

eating miracles
for breakfast
a prayer

breaking news
the sugar pine
bears a cone

tzeva adom
all the poppies
on red alert

holding darkness
light in its palm
the prayer plant

                         digging up the dead
                         blue raptors

Swallowing stones

Another white night and he crosses over. In the midrash, matriarch Sarah dies upon hearing of the Binding. In the midrash, ten thousand tales of Isaac are told.

    small hours
    I check the clockface
    and see my own

grooming the dog
my final jisei

blown-up bus
speaking with the pigeon
more softly

still life
beneath the bodies
a prayer

stopping anytime
I want I reach
for another poem

cold copulars
his empty
side of the bed

fairy lights on the Litani slow-motion aircraft

odd birds in formation my fear

entirely entangled
the bluebottle
tipping

رؤية النفق

رهائن

رهائن

رهائن

tunnel vision
hostages
hostages
hostages

מבט מנהרה

חטופים

חטופים

חטופים

The diamonds are in our hands

Black wind. It's ashy this morning and the speakers nonfunctional. Plenty of amplification, though. I hear what I hear, it's so hard not to. Broadcast on the GoPros. They can see for themselves.

war night never-ending dragonflies into ether

diaphanous day
the razor's edge
of light

this time
thunder
under siege

car inspection
I'm held together
with duct tape

rewilding the shattered glass of a drive-by

days of peace
I check the chamber
and start to pray

reading the news
one fingertip at a time
touch of grief

לאחר המטוס. . . תורמוס

بعد الطائرات...ترمس أرجواني

after the planes . . . purple lupine

Objects in the mirror are closer than they appear

Amid the morning's deflated santas, a reindeer stands. Slim, almost ice. I slow down and read her eyes. Which way, she wants to know, to the North Pole?

light to moderate casualties the sunrise

sweeping
the grave of a soldier
my shadow

the short-lived
needs of the hibiscus
jisei day

back to the bunker
my neighbors'
nightclothes

wartime wildflowers leaning toward the light

Who by fire

It's a funny day for a photoshoot. Airstrikes and all that. But our reservists are home for the moment, and the little ones are getting bigger. So here we are in the forest, laughing as though our lives depended on it. Later, in the tumult of departure, I leave my bag behind. Just a phone and some letters from the kids, but still. We turn the car around, and there it is: a mauled thing. Jackals.

after the infiltration
white wind

winter water above the breakers kintsugi

light comes early now
at the cradle
of the soldier's child

my excuse
to return to the rain
old dog

herald patch
waiting for the war
to spread

first morning
the almond blossoms
practicing light

shofar blast
the staccato
of a new year

in the safe room reaching

always the undertow
a cormorant's blue

festooned year the yellow ribbon on a runway

morning after
in the shape of a missile
clouds

إعادة الرقص
جميع الأسماء الجديدة
مطرّزة

ריקוד מחודש
השמות החדשים
רקומים

dancing again
all the new names
embroidered

The silence of small creatures

Out come the Bibas babies, flare-haired and not as young as they used to be. Both heads on a red cross, first they've seen since captivity. The mother is missing, but so are the others. Difficult to keep families together these days.

white heat burning the desert umber

ceasefire moon
all the stars
just stars

first
last day of the year
of
shiv^wa_r

Glossary

Hamsa: A hand-shaped amulet.

Har Herzl: The site of Israel's national military cemetery.

Hijab: A head covering worn by Muslim women.

Hyrax: A small, furry animal.

Jisei: A death poem.

Kaddish: A prayer traditionally recited for the dead in Judaism.

Kibbutz: An Israeli collective community.

Kintsugi: The traditional Japanese art of repairing ceramics with lacquer and gold.

Litani: The chief river of Lebanon.

Midrash: A genre of Jewish literature that interprets biblical texts.

Shavasana: The resting or restorative pose in yoga.

Shiva: The seven-day period of mourning for first-degree relatives in Judaism.

Shofar: A ram's horn.

Small Stones: Visitors to Jewish cemeteries place small stones on the graves as an act of remembrance.

"The Binding": A story from Chapter 22 of the Book of Genesis.

Tzeva Adom: Hebrew for "red alert."

Wadi: Arabic for a dry valley or stream.

Yahrzeit: The anniversary of a death in Judaism.

Acknowledgments

Grateful appreciation to the following journals and books in which some of these poems previously appeared:

The Pan Haiku Review, bottle rockets, Modern Haiku, NOON: journal of the short poem, Kingfisher, upside down: The Red Moon Anthology of English-Language Haiku 2023, Frogpond, The Heron's Nest, and *Presence.*

Appreciation

Sometime after October 7, I learned a lifechanging lesson: my safe space is gratitude. It is in this spirit that I offer the following brief words of thanks.

The poems in this book could not have been written without the feedback of Alan Summers, haiku teacher extraordinaire. David Jacobs has generously given of his time, talent, and humble humor. Stanford M. Forrester (sekiro) saw what I wanted to say and enabled me to do so. I thank the editors of the journals in which some of these poems have been published.

Many friends have supported my haikuing. Here, I will mention three. Naomi Esses, a fine emerging poet herself, is the mother-muse whose voice is heard on these pages. Claudia Zalta's belief in these poems predated my own. Leah Moses Witmer has, somehow, always been present.

My children and their partners (Hadar and Aviad, Ma'ayan and Hagar, Elishama and Shaked, Adin and Michali) are the ground of this work. My grandchildren are the fruit. And my husband, Simcha Wachtel, has lovingly nurtured the seeds.

About the Author

Sara Tropper lives in Israel with her husband, children, grandchildren and dog. When she is not editing books and articles for scholars, she enjoys losing on the soccer field to her grandsons and writing haiku on the hillside.

About the Artist

David Berger is an award-winning artist and haiku poet. He creates with a variety of media, including sumi ink and Asian brush, the materials used for the interior images of this book. Berger resides in Seattle and recently established a new, larger studio. https://davidaberger.net/

About the Translations

I am thrilled to be working in the English-language haiku tradition. At the same time, I live in Israel—a country whose two official languages are Hebrew and Arabic. The book is dedicated to those who spoke all these languages, and more. May their names be for a blessing.